Queenager

Random brain farts

By

Kirsty Webb

This lil sweet warm cookie is for every Queenager that had an impact on my life.

My mother Jeanette for teaching me how to be lady like, sorry i failed lol. My Nan Edie and Nan Hilda for showing me its possible to be content with my own company. For my Aunty Roz who taught me the value of fun. My aunty Carol for showing me that being me is all good. For Chris who did every single DIY job herself. My sister Stacy for always trusting me, my cousins Rachy, lal n Zo for putting up with my constant tormenting. For Treec my calming farmers wife and nugget for showing me another world. My daughters Cami-Rose and Tyra-Mai for understanding and having patience. To my queens, caz, kate, Kelly, zoe, Emma, sam g, shelbel, Claire H, Lauren G, Sa Rah, claire R Lauren M, sam s. To Keri and Amy for the 'ventures over the venture. For Jennie, rylans 2nd mom and my friend.

The Honorary Queenagers

My boys Conner, Brandon, Rylan and little Elliott. My dad and biggest fan, Tony my sons father Ryan. The lads Lee and Adam

List of brain farts

What is a Queenager

Having your fellow Queenagers back

Climbing a tree in high heels

School attendance

Making peace with me

New laws

What to pack

Valentines mindfulness

Accepting my flaws

Ozone ly joking

The odd identity crisis

Move them hurdles love

The day the earths heart broke

Often embarrassing

Queenage daydreams

Korea maybe

Driving, gimme a Valium

Queenage romance

Make me a boss lady

Watch the boxing

My curious little man

Stockpiling

I wanna get married

What is a Queenager

To be a Queenager, you need to understand exactly what a queenager is. I couldn't find the word Queenager in the dictionary. Only queen-ager on urban dictionary by someone called Lorcrest. He or she claimed it was someone around the same age of the queen! Piss off is it. So i reinvented The word minus the hyphen. I found the word 4 times, even 1 that claimed it was a gay youth or effeminate man! Not 1 description suited such a glamorous word.

I decided to input my own version.

QUEENAGER- a woman with life experience who still knows how to have fun. That was exactly it. A woman who had lived life, possibly a mother, carer or career girl. A mother on benefits or happy sal rolling in the 50 quid notes. A woman who lifts other women, a woman who helps another woman believe in herself. A woman that has been broken enough to truly understand lows, deal with them and then celebrate the highs even if she doesnt have the strength too. Women who have hurt, loved, lost, failed, won, got beaten or succeeded like a boss. Are Queenagers. Women who get it wrong more than they get it right. Women who end up in psych ward. A woman who tries her best. Each and every one having a success rate of 100% at making it through the day. No matter how hard the struggles or stresses.

Honorary Queenager- a man.

I dont mind sharing the definition of Queenager with lorcrest to a certain degree. The queen rocks in many ways and i guess being queen is a bit badass. So im happy to have that reference in there, minus the 'same age' part. But no way will i share with Egypt Thompson! I love the gays. I loved them so much i even grew my own perfect little gay. Gay is cool, middle-aged is not. I loved rainbows, till everytime i wore one i would end up with numbers being popped in my pocket by lovely ladies. I have to endure 3 ladyboys at the magic of Thailand festival 10 times a year, who look more female than me. I allow it though. Gays deserve the rainbow. I would just like the numbers in my pockets to be hot men, not hot women. Eughhh here i go again, off on a tangent, me ma would say. So no, Sorry Egypt. Im sticking to my guns on this one. I have too if im going to save the world.

Having your fellow Queenagers backs

Hands up, i can not drink, i dont know when to stop so i now tend to stick to shandy or spritzers and allow myself 1 proper drink after a meal. Unless i am drinking to get drunk then im hanging over the bar, reeking of fags and booze, waving my bank card at the barman. Whos trying not to make eye contact, making me climb over the bar to stand and tap his shoulder. If im wanting to drink, i go hard or sod off home. Unfortunately i wish i could say that most often i sodded of home, which would be a huge fib. Fortunately for you i went hard.

The Queens were in Marrakech, our second visit that year. This time child free and peak season so we were #lovinglife. We had managed to get the flights and exact same hotel we stayed at in March.

We were there for 1 thing. Relaxation. Caz, Zoe and i had visited the souks the last time we came. I adored wandering around the narrow souk alley ways back in March but it was too much like hard work. Shopping in the markets of marrakech which are known as souks is nothing like shopping in England. Here we wander around clothing shops, finger through rails of clothing with our phone perched ear to shoulder, leisurely swanning down the aisles, owning the floor space like a ballroom dancer, examining things you like or don't like. We have to hunt down sales assistants to ask them 6 questions about something we dont really want after all. We buy or we dont buy. The cashier cant give a flying fuck either way, she stays at her till when we leave.

Marrakech is a Muslim country so we covered up. Caz in three quarter jeans and white round neck t-shirt, zo in jeans with a black tshirt / grey cardigan (bear in mind it gets over 35° inside the souks) i choose a pair of blue and white hareem pants, a white kaftan with a white and pink scarf that i wore over my head to try and blend in (in that gets up i looked like a sore thumb)

The minute we got into the souks we each hit the first shop that caught our eye. I picked up a wooden hand carved elephant and shouted Caz, she did the whole 3 steps back, look, giggle and carried on back to the handbags she was inspecting. I put the elephant back onto the stand and joined Caz at the handbags where i stood having a fag and drink of water.

The guy from the elephant stall came over to me carrying the elephant "you like? He asked

"Yea its beautiful" i said wondering if he was heading off to grab a coffee or something.

"you buy, i give for you nice price" he squeaks at me.

"No i just wanted to show my friend"

"Buy 2 i make best deal in all of marrakech "

"no thank you" i laugh as i hear Caz calling me over, She was standing at the till her arms laden with trinkets doing her best to put them down. the owner off the shop still piling her up.

 "Whats up" I asked her.

I don't want all these bloody things, he keep putting them in my arms. Everytime i try to tell him that I don't want them he follows me and puts something else in my arms". Typical bloody caz. I soon realised that unless you were 100% interested in buying something from the shop you kept your head down, but you definitely do nott ask questions. Sadly Zoe didnt catch on until they had sold her the entire contents of the souks. She got followed around the souks by every single vendor because shes such a friendly chatty gullible type. It was a pretty traumatic experience. Trying to navigate the narrow passageways and avoid little old ladies on fast motorbikes was stressful enough, try keeping an eye on two teenage girls, refusing to wear more than shorts and tiny tank tops because they are 'too hot' and two boys under 10, each with ADHD and full of excitement. Kate had heard enough, so had very little interest in going to the souks anyway. The rest of us were pretty skint, so we were all happy to stay in the all inclusive hotel that was luxurious by our standards. So the hotel which was more than enough Peak season Walmer weather being waited on hand and foot. I I'm getting drunk and technically it wasn't my fault. Yes the Tequila sunrises Moorish but due to the heat ice melted very quick and I didn't taste that nice. Side by side the four of us lay in the sun topping up a factor 50 and sipping tequila sunrises and mojitos. no normally I wouldn't have attempted to drink 6 drinks before the ice melted in around 40 degree heat, but this was my last day and I was on holiday so why not hammer 6 murderous drinks down my mush within 15 minutes. I was wetting my wotsit today i tell ya. I remember getting into the pool, relaxing as the water carried my sozzled up torso, then getting rocked by the odd bob, of course i fell asleep!

 apparently I was asleep for quite a while, the girls having the odd glance at me doing my best impression of a lilo. They only left me with Zoe, who wanted me to get out the pool and get ready for dinner

Caz and Kate had gone upstairs for quick old lady naps. Caz was down first and spotted Zoe trying to get me out of the Pool. They eventually hauled me and my belly onto a sun lounger. I looked like a sealion flipping anda flapping to get myself upright. When i finally managed to erect myself, i decided to jump back in to rub my titties on some random

dudes bald head, really pissing his wife off in the process.
Kate caughtthe tail end of my ass been dragged out of the
pool by Caz and Zoe.

"Thank god you're here" Caz rasped hoarsely.

"She's pissed out of a bloody head" zoe winched.

I remember getting to my feet for the second time, stumbling
a few tappy steps towards the hotel door, it went a tad hazy
then the grass came up and hit me with a keep off the grass
sign. Fair play, the Queen's did try to get me up, but im not
the most delicate of daisies even if im the shortest of the
Queenagers. The stupid pavement kept shaking me , making
me fall run into the bush the other side of the pavement.

I dont remember hitting the bush, only bouncing off. The
baby blue sky slowly coming into view as i landed with a
graceful yet noisy thud. Everyone around the pool made an
'ooooffff' sound in unison. But they kept me safe, them lil
darlins.

Climbing a tree in high heels

Being such a lover of the outdoors, i decided to add a bit
sparkle to our adventure.
Whilr everyone was packing their picnics, i was running
around gathering anything and everything, that could be used
as a fancy dress item.
We all piled into our cars and headed out to our spot in

Ashridge.
We played for a bit.
we ate.
The kids ran off to play, while we nattered away.
I'd forgotten about the bag of dressing up stuff. Id left water
in the boot, so when i opened the boot, i spotted it.
"Iv got a surprise for you ladies " i sang as i danced towards
them.
BOOOOFFFF as the bag hit the ground.
"Whats that" Shelbel asked
"Find out yourself" i told her excitedly.
Woooooooshhh! Shelbel and Sam got there first, closely
followed by Kelly and Michelle.
Vivi did not move. Statuesque she is not, but statue is what
she was as the Queens raided the bag like children.
At first they were hesitant. They just took costumes out,
talked about each one then put them back.
I felt a little sad that each of them had been conditioned by
society to almost avoid fun. So i got up and raided the bag
like i was 5 again.
I think i put on a tutu and a plastic seashell bra and turned the
music up a tad.
I grabbed a hamburger hat and wedged it on Shelbels head.
She giggled like a little girl and asked what i was doing.
"Having fun" i said in a silly voice.
I grabbed a chilli pepper hat and put that on Sams head.
I remember seeing her eyes light up as i did that.
Kel had already cracked on and was dressed in a belly dancer
outfit. Waving her arms around and singing to herself as she
shook her hips.

I was wearing a sexy sailor girl outfit and planted my bum next to Vivi.
Who had now joined it too and was rocking a pizza hat and scarf.
It felt magical.
For a few minutes we became children again.
The sun was shining, the breeze was gentle and warm. We were in the middle of nowhere feeling safe enough to let go a little bit. We decided to go for a quick wander and check on the kids... in costumes.
I had even packed a pair of heeled mules that matches my outfit.
Shelbel was trotting off ahead in her fairy outfit and hiking boots, while i tottered behind in my high heels.
The kids were playing around a few trees and 1 had fallen over "Shel, can you take a pic of me on here please?
"Yea" she said laughing.
I climed up onto the lowest part of the tree, but for some reason decided to keep climbing, and climbing and climbing until i found the perfect spot for a pic.
"Done" Shelbel hooted
"Erm Shel, how can i get down?
Climbing up in heels wasnt too hard. But going down wasnt so easy. Initially i tried so hard to climb down in the heels, but then my mom brain kicked in and i realised that was a very silly thing to do. Shel got 1 of the kids to run back and grab my flip-flops. Which took forever so i climbed the rest of the way barefoot. Cutting and pricking my poor feet to shreds.
Memories made.

School attendance

How many of you have had attendance warning letters for
your kids being off ill 1 time too many?
I chose to send the kids into mainstream, because i didnt
know there was another option back then
but this attendance malarkey is twisting my noodle beyond
spaghetti.
Rylan gets a sticker on a Monday if he has 100% attendance..
There are posters EVERYWHERE explaining the importance
of attendance 'be an attendance superhero' yea sorry kids, you
cant be a superhero if your ill or cant make it in for genuine
reasons. We devote many mothering moons to raising our
sprogs, to be happy in their own skins, only for school and
peers to undo it all, in the name of statistics.
Poor Cami often trots off to school when she's ill, apparently
her attendance may affect her GCSE'S so shes petrified to
stay home just incase.
It seems our school system put attendance before education!
Lets start catering to each individual childs needs, drawing up
personal curriculums instead of a national one.
Anyway peace off im out.

Making peace with me

An old pic popped up on my phone.. i was about 3 when this

pic was taken. So happy and content, very loved by everyone
except herself sadly.
I wish i could spend 1 day with little me.
I'd take me to the highest place i could find and look down
across the miles of countryside "see the world isnt so big
when your standing on the top, get used to it kidda"
Id steal us a boat, lie back and watch the clouds put on a fine
show, brazenly stand up, if we fall in, il easily swim us both
back to shore.
Id take me to the most crowded place i could find.. and put
me on my shoulders so i was the tallest person there. My little
eyes squished by my beaming smile.
"Will that put things right for letting you down? Id ask
"I wouldnt change anything, i want to be just like you when i
grow up" and i meant it.

UBUNTU....I AM BECAUSE WE ARE

New laws.

1. No loud shirts to be worn in built up areas at night.
2. Crisps are to be eaten with the mouth closed.
3. Wear 3 socks on hot days.

4. Cows and camels must stay in the slow lane unless an accident is due to happen.. then they can just go home...

what to pack

Back from seeing vivis shiny new beaut of a bab..
Driving home i think about birth, how we come into the world with nothing and leave the same way..
That's not true..
We come into the world with nothing, no clothing, no knowledge.
A blank canvas..
We can then choose to spend our lives gathering items or memories.
Filling our canvas full of moments we can relive over and over...again and again. No storage, no theft.. yours..
Im gonna leave this earth with my canvas looking like a mandala of the brightest colours ☐ good job really, cos iv got feck all else to leave.

Valentines mindfulness

Its the day of lurve!!
A strange one, but self love isnt easy..
So whether your single, wed or just plain confused..
Remember.. YOUR success rate at gettin through the days is 100%!!

YOU are amazing!!
Being happy loving you isn't an easy tin of beans to find in
the cupboard. Its wedged well high up and too far back for
most. We are all born a blank canvas.. we soak up our
behaviours from those who are around us.
When you stop.. look at the big picture and slow life down..
you see so much more, the smells around you are stronger
and trigger memories to explore to the forefront of your
mind.
The colours brighter, the noises easier to define.
Your in the moment..
That's being mindful..
Putting down your phone and looking into your child's eyes
as they chat away about things that matter to them and things
you couldnt give a flying fumble for, yet listen intently.

Turn off the TV.. get a game out, go kick a football.. walk
barefoot in grass.
We aren't made to sit staring at tiny talking picture boxes ..
Nor sit watching TV.. in silence..
We're social creatures. Who can often avoid everyday
situations cos we fear some ridunclulating things.
Most of which didn't exist 100 yes ago..
Before these crazy insanehorror stories and films filled our
heads with irrational bullshit, we had no fears.
Clowns weren't scary
Alleyways lead you home quicker
Forests places of beauty to explore
Baths don't contain sharks
Wardrobes contain clothes

Under your bed is space..
Etc etc etc
We allow negatives into our heads..
Our heads..
We have control of what goes in to our minds..
And our kids.. what do they see.. is it positive?
Or negative? What's the balance?
I'm learning all of the above.. but the more I learn.. the more
it makes sense..
Law of attraction..
Live positively and positive karma comes along..
Live negative.. karma is negative..
The world's struggling and we need to start making major
changes NOW ..
Rant over..

Accepting my flaws

Ya can keep trying to bring me down.
Yea it shakes me a bit but, it never breaks me.
All my skeletons danced out my closet long ago.. the same
day I stopped wanging stones at others glass houses..
What you see is exactly what your gonna get..
I don't claim to be perfect . But I'm sure as hell proud!
I wound my neck in and got on with my life!!
Found myself in a great place..
Now you want to try and shake me?
Now?

When I'm at my peak?? Ya fool
You have no power over me.. im happy

Am i?
"I just want to be happy"
A phrase I have used.. a phrase we have all used..
The pursuit of happiness shouldn't be a thing!!
Happiness is inside us.. I thought it was bullshudder.. so
decided to take a year out to date me, yea myself, every wave
n ripple of my very own sexy ass. something I had never
done..
What TV shows did I like?
What did I really enjoy?
What made me smile?
Who am I?
What tickles my pink?
Etc, etc, etc...
I pushed myself outside of my comfort zone, I faced fears
(silly ones if I'm honest lol)
But woke every morning and decided on 1 small goal..
Some days, life got in the way. so I decided to make mantras
for busy days..
Pass something blue.. I had to tell myself a positive thing
about myself..
Pass something bright pink.. I had to treat myself to a mini
pampering.. power nap/salt bath/ painted my nails..
I felt a complete numpty smiling at myself if I passed a
mirror..
I often felt like a big mac in a blender, so these little quests
kept my brain focused on the fresh fruity parts of life.

I had a few offers from ineligible bachelors. I feared
becoming dependent once again.. so I gracefully declined and
focused on the squids, me, the zoo, and me garden...
It's been well over a year, since I stopped hunting for
happiness on the outside..
And today it will be 1 year exactly since I found happiness on
the inside of me.
Result?
A much happier Queenage bee and baby bees.

Ozone ly joking

Farts.. thats what my brain ran to first..
Here is my brainfart..
I have a petite little dainty ladylike beaut of a mate.. i wont
name her, your secret is safe ....anywhich..
Her farts are ripper stinkers.. shes a meat eater..
So imagine chillin' next to ya baestie, watching your fave
flick. Who, just as your drifting off, fires a deadly bum bomb
in your direction. Hell yes your gonna take a few bites before
waking up and craving a bacon butty. I can only guess at
what I'd crave if Sarah quaffed just as I'm drifting off, the
sweet scent of green grass and fresh hay filling my nostrils, i
cop a chew of fresh orange and apples with a hint of
raspberry. Not that sarah eats grass or hay. She's human.
Wait, I've never heard or smelled anything quaffy. So she
may indeed be superhuman.

Hmm think I'll go make a cuppa.

The odd identity crisis

Today i am identifying as the prime minister..
All religion is to be banned..all houses of worship are to be turned into community centres.. a few will become safe havens for homeless.. detox centres.. rehabs etc..
Supermarkets will be shut down.. local businesses will thrive..
Yea.. sorry.. you wont be able to get your groceries dropped to your door.. you will have to go out and socialise with local retailers..
Street parties once a month..funded by the money saved from me not having a greedy cabinet..
Schools will scrap the national curriculum..and adopt individual curriculums for each and every student..NO CHILD WILL LEAVE SCHOOL FEELING ANYTHING OTHER THAN AMAZING ABOUT THEMSELVES..
Lessons will be geared towards both academic and none acadamic kids..
Maths and english will be taught..
But life skills will be the major focus of education.
Mindfulness everywhere..
Kids will learn to grow veg and fruit..
Will build things, experiment.. SCHOOL WILL AND SHOULD BE FUN.
Im sticking my middle fingers up at the EU and waving bye bye.

Happy Monday..
Today i am identifying as a 21 year old who wears size 8.
Im also brunette.. yes my hair is a brunette shade of blond..
Oh also.. i can sing. Really well.. singism is becoming a big
problem here..
Simon cowell is a major singist!!
Ohh 1 more.. its sunday again x

Move them hurdles love!

Did you know you can trick your self into getting out of bed
the second the alarm goes off.
Here's how..
So first set your alarm.
Then agree with yourself that as the alarm goes off, you won't
start thinking until your on your feet.

How does it work..
Well as humans have evolved, so has their brains.. the first
part to develop is auto pilot.. or. The computer..
Which stores patterns, behaviours, subconscious things..
Next came the emotional part of the brain.
Unable to be reasonable or rational. A machine fuelled by
emotions.
It's purpose is there to keep you alive..
If someone s trying to kidnap you.. the emotional part would
sense danger and react without. Any thought.
Lastly to develop was the thinking part of the brain. Able to

make decisions, rationalise, be human..
By deciding to not to think until you are on your feet, it kicks
in the 1st brain.. bypassing the emotional brain totally.. and
boom your human brain is now stood up ready to go.
I have BPD.. so learning about my condition has been at the
forefront of my daily life..
My emotional brain is confused.. so i over react .
I'm learning to own situations...
That's always a great place to start when the hurdles seem too
high.

The day the earths heart broke

The day the earth's heart broke.
The earth created man and woman.. the same but different.
2 different races no more..
Yet the earth had to spin towards and away from mother sun.
Resulting in certain parts of the earth being hotter than
others...
This resulted in many humans building a resistance to the
sun.. a rainbow of beautiful skin colours. Admired by the sun,
the earth twirled happily, so proud of the men and women
who created life he fell asleep, confident his creations loved
as he did and left his upkeep in man's hands.
But man and women weren't able to live up to the
expectations that the earth expected of them.
In a panic, man ran, and travelled far and wide..
Fear growing at the unknown..
A man with a soft caramel skin landed in a cold land..

A creature with flaming red hair and soft peach skin, came
out of the trees..a tiny girl..
He felt relief.. she did not know what to feel at the sight of
the man before her..
He who was shaped like daddy, had the same smile as
daddy.. except his hair was soft and bouncy. His skin darker..
not knowing how to react.. the girl screamed.. attracting her
family.
Who came upon the man from the sea..
The girls scream was the first ever scream of fear.. which
filled the ears of everyone around her.
Including the man from the sea..
Who returned her scream of fear..as the family of the girl
returned his fear tenfold and killed him
Fear was born.
Man put up borders, and walls and declared ownership of
lands. Fear had won.
Men feared each other. Wars came and went.
Man came and went..to consumed by fear, to just live on the
earth. Communities deteriorated, man grew lazy, lost belief in
themselves. Took and took from the earth without ever
giving. gardens, now prisons of brown. Isolating us from
neighbours.
Earphones block out society.
Humans stand next to humans and are scared to speak to
them.
Yesterday the earth woke up, starving, sick, in pain,
heartbroken as he looked at his once beautiful body and how
man had let him down..
How fear had conquered love.

That was the day the earth's heart broke

Often embarrassing

My sincere apologies to the 3 young men who were sat on the
double decker bus that just pulled up at the bottom of my
garden..
I did not expect a bus to go past my newly trimmed hedge at
6.30am..
I was hot.. I had just woken up so decided to do my morning
stretch butt nekid in me garden.
I was mid downward dog as the bus made a pft pft gassy
noise.. from beween my legs I saw those poor boys..
I had to swiftly move into the cobra then curled up and rolled
behind the sofa.. But dog poo went in my fucking hair..
I was heaving.. Uchh.. Still uckk am..
But there's a silver lining.
CAN'T GET ANY FUCKING WORSE CAN IT

Queenage daydreams

Some time little achievements mean so much.
Finding silver linings and humour in dark times is often a
battle.
I overslept, the kids were going to be late.
Normally I panic and run and shout..
Today I decided I was going to do the opposite.
I was already late, that could not be changed.

But my attitude could.
I lay back down and breathed for a second..
Then struggled like feck to get out of the quilt that was coccooning me.
And as I stepped out of bed.
I decided I was going to do everything as if I was awake on time.
8.30 I wake up.
8.35 Rylan asks where his shirt is.
8.40 Rylan has eaten, cleaned, spruced and gone.
8.41 sip my coffee and remembered that cam has the dentist today at 2pm.
Boom
8.43 write cami a note to be excused from school at 1.30pm and casually fibbed that she was late due to trying to get an appointment. (I was on hold for 20 mins yest, so I'm only moulding a Lil lie☐)
8.52 cami and I are in the car..I'm driving, she's in the back like the perfect Lil princess being chauffeured around, ear phones on.
9.02 cams now in school.
It's now 9.30 and I am back to where I always am at 9.30..
Except, today was an adventure.
May your Wednesdays be epic and awesome.
May you find the silver linings every time.
Turn your day over to the universe and let it do its thang, you get your feet up.

Woah, so my 14 year old told me a year ago that she wanted to go and study in Korea.
I told her if she felt the same way a year on, I would look into it seriously.
Her enthusiasm has grown, she has been learning Korean, sending me link after link on exchange programmes and is more eager than she was a year ago.
Now if any of you know my kids, you'll know that cam is the quietest, most sensible of them all.
Yet that quiet little girl hasn't shut up about Korea for a year. She is determined and my jeez she's shouting loud.

She is 14.. 14..a baby.. My baby, but I have never seen her this enthusiastic about anything before.
So I am looking into the exchange programmes that she has sent me, tears in my eyes at how grown up she is. Cant do much without any work though.
I'm gutted. I feckin love my job.
I don't know any other 41 year old that can get em up as fast as I can.
I'm proud of that fact.
I can boast about all the erections iv been a part of, and unlike most middle aged women, I get to stand on the erections sometimes.
When it's windy I do struggle to get the covers on the bigger erections, it's always a really tight squeeze but I toggle it down around the base to make sure that bad boy stays on tight.

I don't like staking down, it's far too much banging and
forcing for my liking.
I leave that for the boys to do together and I fiddle with my
box of drapes or play with my toggles while I watch them.
We usually all finish at the same time, tidy up then go home..
Ahh strawberry fieldz I miss thee

Driving, gimme a valium

Old drivers. Let's get them a load more ring and rides and
retest the coffin dodgers, who btw are allowed to drive small
lorries!
Oh the idea of a granny dogger flashed through my jellypot.
I wanna wash my mind!!!!!!!

Motorway lessons need to be compulsory..
The middle lane hoggers crawl right up my butt and twist my
intestines.. Its to overtake!!! OVERBASTARDTAKE!!!!!!!!!
.
Not cos you're too stoopid to know how to speed up or slow
down at oncoming feeder lanes!!
You keep your mother fucking ass in the slow lane..
The one on the left... You decide on your speed and go, if you
are slowed by the cunt in front..
Then you can over take!!! Which means go past for them wot
is daft.
Then you stick you and your fuckwingle car back into the
sloooooooow lane..

We don't need 27 lane motorways if you know how to use them!!!!!!

Queenage Romance

2 years ago I met someone and began a love affair.. I knew this person was the one I was looking for.
When I felt ugly, they told me I was beautiful.
When I was sad, they made me happy
When I was hyper, they knew how to calm me.
The first year wasn't a honeymoon.
We had to get to know each other, we rowed lots, disagreed often. But over time, I believed in them, allowed my barriers to come down, accepted what was and accepted what I couldn't change.
I learned to stop and look at everything in detail.
They taught me how to accept and love myself.
How to avoid spiralling into a police cell, and instead just stay exactly where I was, and be in the moment, step out of my emotional mind and use my rational mind instead.
Iv known this person my whole life, avoided them, believing they were beneath me, a wrong un..
So I moved, they followed, I moved again they followed again..
Wherever I went there they were.
So I gave in and allowed them into my life.
Wanna know who?

Me.

I'm gonna run for prime minister.
If elected I promise too.
1.Rob from the rich and liberate the poor.
2. Send the national curriculum up to mars and bring in individual curriculums, Taylored to enhance each child's strengths.
3. Education will be fun.
A kid can't learn if it's not interested, yet we still plonk them into lessons that they can't grasp, which lowers their self esteem.
Schools will offer a variety of practical subjects and life skills.
Maths and English will be taught via the fun lessons.
4. Teach kids mindfulness and how to be in the moment to prevent mental health issues in adulthood.
5. Doctors and nurses will receive a hefty pay rise, which will come from the Royal allowances
6. The BBC and its annoying door knockers will be banned. (Screw the tv licence...)
7. Income tax will be abolished for those earning under 1 million pa.
8. Every family will receive a food allowance, no one goes hungry.
9. Pool every resource into combating/preventing mental illness.

10. Still deciding

So don't forget to add my name to the ballot papers when you
go and vote.

Watch the boxing

You got AJ, classy robe, swish entrance, nice clean shorts
and tidy.
Or Ruiz, Who waddled in dressed like a sausage roll with a
mouldy tip!
Then strips off to reveal the value shorts his mama brought
him are in fact his older brothers swimming shorts complete
with badges and haven't been washed. They seem to be
twisting too!
3 rounds in his back gets hungry and attempts to eat his
shorts, which are now so twisted he has 3 camel toes.
Don't get me started on the foot wear. He could of asked his
old dear for a new pair for fuck sake! AJ will win I predict

My curious little man

Yesterday my 7yr old made me realise a few things.
We go through 4/6 pints of milk a day.
That's 365 plastic bottles in the bin.
We use 1 bottle of shampoo and 2 bottles of conditioner a

week. That's 150 plastic bottles in the bin.
We get through 4/8 bottles of water, juice etc..
That's 2920 plastic bottles in the bin!!
When I showed my son a collection of 20 bottles, he was able
to understand that we could fill our lounge and dining room
with rubbish.

He asked me where it went.
I had no idea.
Most of the bottles are recyclable but each year 60 billion
bottles end up in landfill.
I explained how landfills work.
And told him that houses are built on top of the rubbish.
Ewwww I hope they don't try and grow veg!!!

He was shocked.
Why wasn't I? Conditioned to the bullshit I guess lol.

I want to make changes.
I am going to get myself a milk man□□.
I'm going to make my own shampoo and conditioner.
Which is really easy.
I'm going to research home made cleaning products and reuse
the bottles I currently have.

I guess that's my new years resolution, I am taking
responsibility for my actions and vow to make steps to save
the planet in a small way.

Elliott would like to ask a few of you to make a change.

Just 1 small change.

Try one of these?
Get your milk delivered in glass bottles.
Buy cans not bottles.
Turn off the tap when cleaning your teeth.
Don't flush the loo every time.
Recycle old clothes.
Get the pop man back! Who didn't love giving back 6 glass bottles and getting 60p???!!
Pubs, switch to glass bottles, add 20p deposit to the price..
Boom.... Kids will be bringing the bottles back....
Turn off your lights.
Share a bath□□ (I'm waiting for me milkman □)
Or be badass and make your own products at home.

Elliott inspired me BIG TIME!
So I am paying it forward.
If i inspire you, please pay it forward

Here is a link to find your milkman.
https://findmeamilkman.net/

Stockpiling

Is it selfish?
Fuck yea it is.. but that's what happens when the media starts scaring folk with maybes and what ifs.
I have always stock piled.. my mom did, me nans did..
They were after war babies and knew hardship and genuine "going without"
When i was about 10 i went to a friends house for tea..
Her mom picked us up and asked me what i wanted to eat..
I think it was fish and chips.. so we then went to the shop and brought the ingredients..
I only remember how empty the cupboards were because we hid in them.
I later told my mom off for always having stuff in the cupboard.
As i grew up i understood that some people lived day to day or week to week and some, like my lot, lived just incase to just incase.
I found my own mojo re the issue and tend to try and keep 2 weeks ahead of food, toiletries etc.. and thats what I've done my whole adult life.
Id happily share what i had if someone i knew needed something i had.
I dont see my "stockpiling" as selfish.
I see it as being sensible..
Oh if ya want a loo roll, im doing a friend discount.. 50% off £14 per roll yea joke..
Im here to save your ass.. limited to 2 per friend

why does my boy only want to spend time with me when his
bumbum keeps chugging out love puffs i waited all day to
make dragon eggs.
How do you enjoy quality time with ya sprogs when every
few mins a whiff scooches over and knocks you senseless???

2 minute mindfulness

You will need
1 small sweet (haribo, malteser, chewit etc..
A quiet space.
2 minutes of your time.

Get comfortable in your quiet place (kids love this 1)

Now take your sweet and look at it, squish it, pull it, poke it...
take your time examining it.

When your ready, smell it.

does it make a noise?

Now pop it into your mouth and roll it around your mouth,
noticing any bumps, lumps or ridges..
Is it melting, it it sour or sweet?
Is it dissolving, how does it taste?

When your ready, chew as normal..

Done

I wanna get married

Not because i have met the love of my life, i just want the wedding. My other 2 weddings weren't made of crispy fresh dreams like this one. Feck no!

The first one was a really lovely day, but mu mom got a dodgy relation to make my wedding dress. I was 5 months preggers with Conner, so asked for a dress that enhanced my bump. The dosey cow made ke a dress that not only hid my precious bump, it made me look fat.

I wanted to cry. My mom asked me to wear it so i woukdny offend the relative. Being a good girl i did. Looking back i should have taken that vile dress and smothered this bleedin precious relative of me ma's. Dad and i raced down the traditional parquet floor of St Johns church. I cant remember the wedding, but the reception wasnt bad, Bridgnorth leisure centre for buffet and disco.

The second one was in bridgnorth a registry office. I only remember realising that i had got married at both ends of Bridgnorth, and the disco at the Conservative club in Reans.

This wedding would be on a much grander scale.

I would hire a B and B on some farm out in the middle of the stix from Friday to Monday, erecting 4 huge marquees a stage in 1 field.

Yurts , old gypsy caravans and bonfire in another

The Friday evening i would welcome my guests to my hen party or bachelorette for you across the pond. There will be a fair in 1 field with a carousel decorated with giant unicorns and dragons gliding up and down as they gently spin round.

The waltzer seats giant cupcakes with every topping you can imagine. A big wheel laden with pumpkin carriages lit up the back of the field.

Coconut shys, shoot em up, water blasters and a 1920s penny arcade sprinkled over the last empty spots and voilà candy floss in every colour, on sticks forms a giant rainbow backdrop as the sun starts to dunk.

The wedding would be me dancing up an aisle of pink sparkly rose petals barefoot in a kaftan towards a mahoosive statue of mother earth made from flowers and Kanye West.

Who asks me "do you kirsty webb agree to always have your own back?

"FUCK YES" id say before high fiving him and starting a flash mob back up the aisle.

The reception would be under a black sky sprinkled with stars around a round wooden table which lifted us all up 8 metres off the ground and span us gently as we ate. We would watch Ye on stage and i do a rendition of jump around with house of pain and Brian May .

Queen headline the night with Freddie and Adam, which pleases both old and young.

I go down as the first woman in history to marry herself.

Hmm maybe i could be the first to divorce also?

www.ingramcontent.com/pod-product-compliance
Lightning Source LLC
Chambersburg PA
CBHW081408130726
47998CB00011B/3116